NOT-FOR-PARENTS

CHINA

Everything you ever wanted to know

Scott Forbes

CONTENTS

HANDS UP IF YOU'RE LOOKING FORWARD TO THIS!

GOT ROOM FOR ME IN YOUR LUGGAGE?

'SNO JOKE VISITING IN WINTER!

LET'S TAKE IT FROM THE TOP!

IT ALL LOOKS GOOD FROM UP HERE!

COME ON DOWN! ANOTHER WORLD AWAITS...

REMEMBER: ALWAYS TRAVEL LIGHT!

NOT-FOR-PARENTS

THIS IS NOT A GUIDEBOOK. And it is definitely Not-for-parents.

IT IS THE REAL, INSIDE STORY about
one of the world's most exciting countries – China.
In this book you'll hear fascinating tales about ancient empires,
martial arts, the discovery of gunpowder and the first cup of **tea**.

Check out cool stories about **ice sculptures,** dust storms,
bloodthirsty warriors and **dragons**. You'll find acrobats, **fighting
crickets,** futuristic buildings and some seriously **weird snacks**.

This book shows you a **CHINA** your parents
probably don't even know about.

DESCENDANTS OF THE DRAGON

Flashing fearsome fangs and talons, they frown at you from rooftops, loom above you on walls, stare at you from doorways and peer out of porcelain pots – dragons are everywhere in China. In the West they might be seen as evil beasts, but the Chinese believe they bring good luck – Chinese people even refer to themselves as the 'descendants of the dragon'. So don't be afraid: those scaly, scary-faced, sharp-clawed critters are there to help!

IT'S MY FLAMING BALL!

High five
Some dragons might appear to be waving – showing off their credentials more like! Emperors decreed that only imperial dragons should have five toes. Dragons associated with commoners and foreigners had to have fewer.

SEE: FIVE AND FIVE! THAT'S ER...EH, HANG ON, IS IT NINE?

Staying on side
Chinese farmers never want to fall foul of dragons, for dragon gods are said to control the seas and weather. A well-timed offering to the gods might just ensure a good harvest!

THE FANTASTIC FOUR

The azure dragon is one of four awesome mythical creatures associated with the seasons and stars. The other three are the fearsome white tiger, the splendid vermilion phoenix and, er, the black tortoise.

High security
Plonk a dragon or two on a temple roof and demons won't darken the door. Or so the theory goes.

NO, IT'S MINE!

AW, HANG ON GUYS, WAIT FOR ME!

HOW LONG IS THIS RACE GOING TO DRAG ON?

Getting ahead
Did you know that racing dragons is a 2000-year-old pastime? Admittedly they're in the form of wooden boats with carved dragon-head prows. Just as well dragons are said to like water!

COME ON, SLOW COACH!

How to train a dragon?
The best way is to assemble a team of 30 to 50 people then make a wood-and-fabric dragon up to 70m (230ft) long. Hold it aloft on long poles and coordinate your movements so the dragon seems to move naturally. Do it well and you might end up performing at New Year festivals.

WANT MORE?

Dragon myths ☆ http://traditions.cultural-china.com/en/212Traditions1324.html

ONE AT A TIME, PLEASE!

Let's hope you're a people person because China is one packed place. It has the world's biggest population (1.3 billion) and is home to nearly one in five of all the people on Earth. In 1978, the government decided that the country was getting so crowded that from then on each family could have only one child. That slowed population growth, but more than 300 million babies have been born since – as many people as live in the entire United States!

OI! WAKE UP AND MOVE ALONG. MORE COMING THROUGH!

About 50,000 babies are born in China every day – roughly 35 a minute.

Saltwater sardines
Fancy a quiet swim? Well, you'd best avoid this saltwater swimming pool in the city of Suining in Sichuan Province. Up to 10,000 people pack the pool every day in summer and more than one million take a dip here each year.

WORLD POPULATION

CHINA 19.3%

REST OF WORLD 58.9%

INDIA 17%

USA 4.8%

HAVE YOU GOT MY RUBBER DUCK DOWN THERE?

GETTING AWAY FROM IT ALL

f you want room to move, head west, where huge areas have few or even no people. Of course, that's mainly because they are freezing cold mountains and scorching, sandy wastelands like the Gobi Desert. Not exactly inviting!

AH, PEACE AT LAST! NOW WHERE DID I PUT MY WATER BOTTLE?

GET OUT OF MY WAY!

It's all about me!
Some people think the one-child policy has resulted in a generation of spoiled children with little idea of how to interact with others. The Chinese call these kids 'little emperors' or 'little empresses'.

OKAY, I CAN SEE IT NOW. TURN RIGHT, DAD.

When push comes to shove
Personal space is at a premium in cities like Shanghai. Vast crowds throng the streets and you'll have to jostle for space – never mind a seat – on trains and buses.

WANT MORE?

Latest population figures ✶ www.chinatoday.com/data/china.population.htm

GAME ON!

Chess and chequers, dominoes and cards, yo-yos and shuttlecocks – in China there's always a game on somewhere. You'll see people playing in homes, streets and playgrounds, cafes, parks and gardens. Many games date back hundreds of years and have been exported to other parts of the world. Some might be familiar, but others are like nothing you've ever seen before!

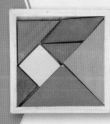

Shape shifting

You don't need to know any Chinese to play tangram. Simply use the pieces to make shapes including animals, buildings and people.

BRINGING THAT LITTLE STOOL WAS SUCH A CRAFTY MOVE!

4998, 4999... TIME TO CHANGE LEGS

Chinese chess

First played around AD 700, *xianqi* is a strategy game similar to Western chess. The contest represents a battle between two armies, each trying to capture the opposing general.

On the tiles

Mahjong is like a card game played with tiles instead of cards. It became a craze in the West in the 1920s after it was introduced to the United States by Joseph Park Babcock.

Look, no hands!

Jianzi, or kick shuttlecock, dates back to the 5th century BC. Players have to keep the shuttlecock in the air using their feet and any other parts of their body – except their hands.

The popular Western game of Chinese chequers is not Chinese but was invented in Germany in 1892.

In a spin
A Chinese yo-yo consists of a pair of sticks joined by a long string, along which you whirl wooden discs. Skilled players wow spectators with dazzling tricks. In the West, the game is known as diabolo.

3, 2, 1...READY FOR LIFT-OFF!

Black and white
Go is the world's oldest board game, dating back at least 4000 years. The aim is to surround your opponent's pieces with yours.

N THE RED CORNER...

ince the Middle Ages, crickets have been bred to o battle. Urged on by spectators, two crickets push, ostle and jab until one backs down. Champions hange hands for big money.

OKAY, YOU HIT ME WITH A RIGHT AND I'LL GO DOWN. LET'S GET THIS OVER WITH QUICKLY.

WANT MORE?

Learn how to play mahjong ☆ http://mahjong.uchicago.edu/home.shtml

KEEPING IT IN THE FAMILY

Confused by Ming and Qing? Unsure about Song and Han? You need to get to grips with the dynasties. Until 1911, China was governed by a series of ruling families, or dynasties, that each provided one or more emperors. Of course, some emperors were more successful – or meaner and madder! – than others, and there were periods of bloodshed and chaos between dynasties. But it went, more or less, like this…

All together now

The long-lasting Han Dynasty helped the Chinese start to feel like one big family. Today 91 per cent of Chinese consider themselves Han people. And that makes them the biggest ethnic group on Earth!

Xia Dynasty, 2200–1700 BC	Shang Dynasty, 1600–1046 BC	Zhou Dynasty, 1046–256 BC	Qin Dynasty, 221–206 BC	Han Dynasty, 206 BC–220 AD	Jin Dynasty, AD 266–420

THE FIRST EMPEROR

The first ruler to unite China, Qin Shihuang was a tough taskmaster with little time for the opinions of others. He burned all historical records except his own and executed 460 scholars who had dared to criticise him.

Qin on film

Among the many books and films based on Qin Shihuang and his dynasty is the 2002 movie *Hero*, starring martial arts expert Jet Li.

NICE DAY? DID I SAY IT WAS A NICE DAY? DID I?

The one and only Wu

Initially a concubine, Wu Zetian won Tang emperor Gaozong's heart after disposing of her main female rivals by having them beaten, their hands and feet cut off and finally drowned in barrels of wine. In AD 690 she deposed her own son and became China's only female emperor.

LIKE TO GIVE ME A HAND?

LET'S SEE: 'THERE WAS A YOUNG MAN FROM BEIJING...'

Top marks

An impressive military leader, 18th-century Qing emperor Qianlong was also a star scholar. He oversaw the publication of a four-million-page compendium of knowledge and wrote more than 40,000 poems.

Southern & Northern Dynasties, AD 420–581	Sui Dynasty, AD 581–618	Tang Dynasty, AD 618–907	Song Dynasty, 960–1279	Yuan Dynasty, 1279–1368	Ming Dynasty, 1368–1644	Qing Dynasty, 1644–1911

I'M A VERY ᐯVANCED FISH!

Last of all

Imagine being made emperor aged two. And then being told at six that your dynasty is over (you'd have a tantrum, wouldn't you?). That's what happened to Puyi, last emperor of China. Later he spent 10 years in prison before ending his life as an ordinary citizen.

ME? EMPEROR? GREAT, I LIKE PLAYING SOLDIERS!

During the Song Dynasty, China was the world's most advanced civilisation.

WANT MORE?

Find out about the early days ✫ www.ancientchina.co.uk

LOOKS GOOD ON PAPER

It's one of the handiest inventions ever. You can carry things in it, write and draw on it, use it for wrapping gifts, even fashion aeroplanes out of it. Understandably, Europeans were pretty pleased with themselves when they worked out how to make paper in the 13th century. Little did they know that the Chinese had beaten them to it – by more than 1000 years!

HMM, MIGHT TRY ADDING SOME OLD SOCKS NEXT TIME.

Secret recipe

About 2000 years ago, Chinese scholars had to write on strips of bamboo and sheets of silk. Fortunately for them, in AD 105 a court official called Cai Lun created the first-ever paper, using mashed up mulberry bark, plant matter, old rags and bits of fishing nets. Quite a concoction!

JUST A TRIM, PLEASE!

Jianzhi, the art of paper cutting, dates back to the 6th century.

Bottoms up

Paper is used to make traditional Chinese lanterns. The medium-sized red ones are known, for obvious reasons, as tomato lights. The smallest type is called a baby's bottom lantern.

aking their mark

he Chinese devised various methods of rinting onto paper. The *Diamond Sutra*, a uddhist text, is the world's oldest printed ook, dating from AD 868.

FIT FOR AN EMPEROR

The first-ever reference to toilet paper comes from a 6th-century Chinese scholar who wrote that he dared not use pages printed with classical texts 'for toilet purposes'. By the late 1300s, huge quantities of toilet paper were being made in China, including special extra-large, perfumed sheets for the royal family.

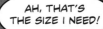

AH, THAT'S THE SIZE I NEED!

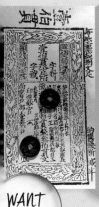

Hey big spenders

In the 9th century, merchants got sick of hauling heavy bundles of coins around, so they wrote each other notes promising to pay up later. The idea caught on and in the 10th century the Song government issued the world's first paper money.

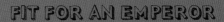

WANT MORE?

Have a go at paper cutting ✴ http://papercutting.net

HOW TO MAKE PEOPLE LOOK SMALL

As emperor you want your subjects to feel small and powerless and make yourself look big and godlike. One way to do that is build a humungous palace – and keep it all to yourself. Clearly this was Emperor Yongle's thinking when in 1406 he ordered the construction of the Forbidden City. It became the imperial residence for the next 500 years – and no one but the royal family, trusted advisers and nervous official visitors was ever allowed in.

9986...DOES A CUPBOARD COUNT ER, WHERE WAS I? AW, NO!

Plenty of room
Built by one million workers over 14 years, the Forbidden City has at least 800 buildings and 9000 rooms – some say 9999. Do you think anyone has ever counted them?

I'VE GOT MY EYE ON YOU!

WHAT, IT EVEN HAS ITS OWN RIVER?!

Scary entrance
Imagine you're a humble scholar on your way to meet Yongle. You enter the palace via a huge gate guarded by fierce stone lions – no doubt already feeling that little bit smaller!

All alone on a sea of stone
Once inside, you have to cross one of five marble bridges over the Golden Stream and hike across the vast Outer Court to the Supreme Harmony Gate. And then there's still a way to go!

POSITIVELY NO ENTRY!

I LIKE TO SPREAD ESELF ABOUT.

Hall of Heavenly Purity
This was Yongle's bedroom, so no way would you have got near here! Later emperors used it as a reception hall.

The Forbidden City's main courtyard can hold 100,000 people.

Top of the pile
Emperor Yongle was the third Ming ruler – and a really, really BIG guy.

The Imperial Garden
Forever out of bounds to all but royals, this was where the emperor liked to relax.

Seat of power
An energy-sapping trek across yet another huge courtyard leads to the Hall of Supreme Harmony, still China's biggest wooden building. Inside, the emperor occupies a colossal throne. By this time, you're quaking in your boots and probably too befuddled to speak or even remember why you're here. Oh dear.

WANT MORE?

The Forbidden City is now a museum ✫ www.dpm.org.cn

ALL THE TEA IN CHINA

A fine day in China, 2737 BC. Emperor Shennong is travelling through countryside. At a rest stop, his servants bring him his usual drink of boiled water. As he reaches for it, a puff of wind drops a few leaves into the cup. He watches the water turn brown then takes a sip. 'Not bad,' he thinks, 'I might try this again.' Almost 5000 years on from this fabled first cuppa, China is the biggest producer of what is, after water, the world's most popular drink.

Black tea leaves

Beginning to brew

However it was discovered, tea was being consumed in China by 1000 BC, mainly for medicinal purposes or as food. Tea drinking was widespread by the 7th century AD.

COFFEE FOR ME!

CAN'T WAIT FOR OUR TEA BREAK.

TEAHOUSE ETIQUETTE

Visiting a teahouse is a great way to experience traditional Chinese culture. But remember:

- ☆ Use two hands to lift your cup.
- ☆ Don't ask for sugar or milk.
- ☆ Drink slowly and savour the flavour.
- ☆ Don't place the cup, lid and saucer on the table separately, as this indicates you are unhappy with the service – unless you are, of course!

High tea

Shanghai's famous Huxinting Teahouse has hosted heads of state including US President Bill Clinton and Queen Elizabeth II.

Man or myth?

A legendary figure, Shennong may or may not have existed. Often depicted as a rather scary looking guy, he is said to have introduced farming to China, as well as 365 types of medicinal plant.

YUM, I THINK I'LL CALL THIS LIQUORICE.

Some wild tea trees in China are nearly 3000 years old.

Bloomin' lovely!

Teas are also made from flowers and herbs. Flower teas are served in glass vessels so you can see the dried flower slowly 'bloom' in the boiling water.

Don't try this at home

Pouring tea this way could get very messy!

I'LL BEND OVER BACKWARDS TO PLEASE MY CUSTOMERS.

WANT MORE?

Learn more about the history and spread of tea drinking ☆ www.tea.co.uk

ARE YOU A RAT?

Or perhaps a monkey, or a rooster?
Not sure? Then you'd better
consult the Chinese zodiac. In
China, everyone is associated with
1 of 12 animals, depending on
their year of birth. Each animal has
certain characteristics, which are
said to be passed on to the
people born in that year.
The zodiac also tells you
which other animals
you'll get on with and
which you should avoid
– so check out your
friends and family too.

> NO, REALLY, I'M A RABBIT!

> IT'S MY BIG YEAR, SO MAKE ME LOOK GORGEOUS.

> YEP, I'M AHEAD OF THE PACK, HEH, HEH...

RABBIT

Year of birth: 1963, 1975, 1987, 1999, 2011

Character: Kind, sensitive, affectionate

Compatible with: Pigs, dragons, goats

Steer clear of: Rats, tigers

TIGER

Year of birth: 1962, 1974, 1986, 1998, 2010

Character: Confident, brave, volatile

Compatible with: Dogs, horses, monkeys

Steer clear of: Goats,.oxen

OX

Year of birth: 1961, 1973, 1985, 1997, 2009

Character: Loyal, independent, hardworking

Compatible with: Rats, roosters, snakes

Steer clear of: Tigers, horses

RAT

Year of birth: 1960, 1972, 1984, 1996, 2008

Character: Charming, curious, ambitious

Compatible with: Dragons, monkeys, oxen

Steer clear of: Horses, rabbits

A warm welcome
China marks the New Year with
colourful festivities – these guys
are celebrating the Year of the
Dragon in 2012. The Chinese year
starts in late January, so people
born in January are linked to
the previous year's animal.

Pole position
It's said that the Buddha
held a race to decide
the order of the animals
in the zodiac, and the
rat won by hitching a
lift on the ox's back
then leaping in
front at the finish.

PIG

Year of birth: 1971, 1983, 1995, 200

Character: Giving, noble, trusting

Compatible with: Goats, dragons, pi

Steer clear of: Snakes

DRAGON
Year of birth: 1964, 1976, 1988, 2000, 2012
Character: Powerful, intelligent, fortunate
Compatible with: Rats, pigs, rabbits
Steer clear of: Dragons, oxen

SNAKE
Year of birth: 1965, 1977, 1989, 2001, 2013
Character: Thoughtful, careful, determined
Compatible with: Roosters, oxen
Steer clear of: Pigs, snakes

HORSE
Year of birth: 1966, 1978, 1990, 2002, 2014
Character: Energetic, independent, adventurous
Compatible with: Dogs, tigers, goats
Steer clear of: Rats, monkeys, oxen

GOAT
Year of birth: 1967, 1979, 1991, 2003
Character: Sincere, artistic, generous
Compatible with: Pigs, rabbits, horses
Steer clear of: Tigers, roosters, oxen

The Five Elements
In turn, each animal is also associated with what the Chinese call the Five Elements or life forces — wood, fire, earth, metal and water. For example, 2004 was the year of the wood monkey. Together the 12 animals and 5 elements create a 60-year cycle.

Intelligent?

MONKEY
Year of birth: 1968, 1980, 1992, 2004
Character: Outgoing, fun-loving, intelligent
Compatible with: Rats, monkeys, dragons
Steer clear of: Horses

ROOSTER
Year of birth: 1969, 1981, 1993, 2005
Character: Quick-thinking, efficient, honest
Compatible with: Snakes, oxen, pigs
Steer clear of: Roosters, goats

DOG
Year of birth: 1970, 1982, 1994, 2006
Character: Faithful, careful, supportive
Compatible with: Horses, tigers, pigs
Steer clear of: Dragons

WANT MORE?

Check out precise calendar dates and more ☆ www.chinesezodiac.org

THE TERRIBLE TARTARS

HAVE I GOT YOUR EAR?

In the early 1200s, they suddenly swept out of Central Asia and carved out one of the biggest empires the world has ever seen. Fearsome and ferocious, the Mongols destroyed everything in their path. Terrified Europeans called them 'dog-faced Tartars' – meaning, essentially, devils from hell – while the Chinese referred to them as rootless savages. Barbarians they might have been, but soon they had most of Asia on its knees.

Grisly Genghis

Founder of the Mongol Empire, Genghis Khan is a candidate for the title of 'Baddest Man Ever'. He and his troops razed city after city. Genghis liked to keep a tally of the dead by having his soldiers take an ear from each victim.

Turn and run

A favourite Mongol trick was to have a small group of horsemen ride out and taunt the enemy, then turn and run. Feeling pretty cocky, their opponents would follow, only to find themselves ambushed – and obliterated – by a giant Mongol force.

In 1241, the Mongols were about to conquer Europe, but their leader Ögödei died so they turned round and went home.

OT WHAT T TAKES?

fe as a Mongol warrior wasn't a bag of booty, and you eeded certain qualities and kills to survive.

HOW'S THIS? GRR!

Horsemanship
The Mongols practically lived in the saddle, riding for weeks on end and sleeping on the ground.

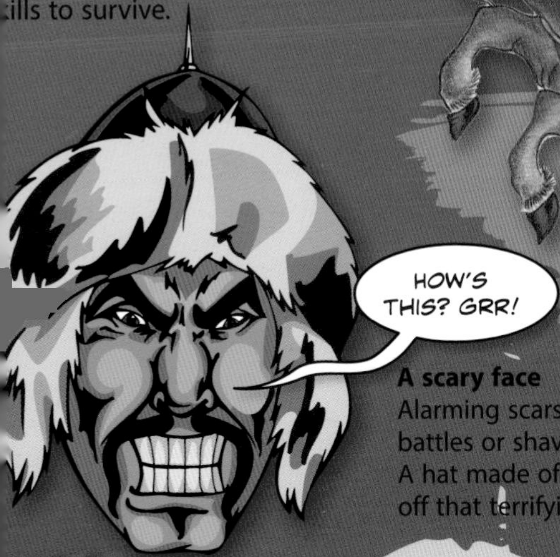

A scary face
Alarming scars, whether from battles or shaving, were essential. A hat made of dog skin topped off that terrifying 'dog-faced' look.

China is ours!
The Mongols seized northern China in 1234. Under Genghis's grandson, Kublai Khan, they conquered the rest of the country and in 1279 founded the Yuan Dynasty.

ARE WE THERE YET?

The high life
In China, Kublai proceeded to live it up in fabulous palaces. He even went into battle in the equivalent of a luxury tank – a pavilion atop four armoured elephants.

WANT MORE?

It's thought that the Mongols wiped out between 30 and 60 million people.

FLYING HIGH

Is that a bird? Is it a plane? Or is it…?
Most likely it's a kite. Kites were first
flown in China about 3000 years ago
and kite-flying remains a hugely
popular pastime. At almost any time
and almost anywhere – in city parks
and squares, in open fields and on
beaches – you're likely to see all kinds
of colourful shapes soaring, swooping
and diving overhead. So watch out!

First cut
In ancient China, kite flyers would glue
pieces of glass and pottery onto their
kite strings. Then they would launch
their kites and duel to see who could
cut the other's kite string first.

Going up!
When powerful, warm air currents are rising,
a strong kite can lift a person. So-called
man-lifting kites were being used in China
by the 13th century, for checking weather
conditions – and for fun!

Sky train

Kite trains consist of numerous small kites joined by a cord. Some are more than 100m (330ft) long and include up to 200 small kites.

Early kite flyers attached pipes, whistles and strings – even miniature harps – to kites so they would make a musical sound as they flew.

Light for flight

Even 3000 years ago, China had ideal materials for making kites: light but strong bamboo canes and sheets of silk. From the 6th century onwards, kites were also made with paper.

KITE CENTRAL

The city of Weifang in eastern China is regarded as the kite capital of the world. Each year in April it hosts a kite festival that attracts thousands of competitors and enthusiasts from around the globe.

COME ON, IT'S EASY, JUST FLAP YOUR WINGS!

WANT MORE?

Learn how to fly a kite ☆ www.drachen.org/learn/kite-basics

CITIFICATION!

China is booming and millions of people are hot-footing it from the country to the city to work in factories, offices and shops – between 15 and 20 million of them every year! As a result, towering apartment blocks, massive housing estates and even entire new cities are sprouting all over the country at an incredible rate.

Mass exodus
In the old days most Chinese lived in rural areas – as recently as 1950 the countryside was home to almost 90 per cent of the population. Today more than half of all Chinese are city slickers.

WHERE DID EVERYONE GO?

More people live in the city of Shanghai than in the whole of Australia.

The changing face of China
Between 2005 and 2025, China's city-dwelling population is expected to grow by 350 million. That's more than all the citizens of the United States!

1950	11%	89%
2030	70%	30%

■ People living in cities ■ People living in the country

LET'S HOPE THAT LIFT KEEPS WORKING.

Not so fast!

Kangbashi, in the booming northern mining district of Ordos, is a high-tech city made to house a million workers. The only problem is hardly anyone wants to live there! So far, most of the region's people have chosen to stay put in their villages and Kangbashi remains a ghost town.

The high life

By 2030, more than one billion Chinese will call a city home. With land space limited, the only way for city housing is up!

HI-HO, HI-HO, IT'S OFF TO WORK WE GO!

On the move

Cities are swelled further by ranks of temporary migrant workers – around 200 million of them. During holiday periods they throng railway stations heading to and from the country.

JUST PASSING THROUGH!

PICKING UP THE PACE

The rate of city growth in China is truly phenomenal. No other country can keep up. And who'd want to? The construction costs alone are colossal.

Building big

More than 50,000 new skyscrapers will be built in China by 2025 – the equivalent of 10 New Yorks, covering an area the size of Switzerland.

Shanghai skyline

Million-people cities

China already has 170 cities with more than one million inhabitants and will have about 220 by 2025. Europe currently has 35 cities that big, the United States just 9.

China 170 cities

Europe 35 cities

USA 9 cities

WANT MORE?

From 1013 to 1127, Kaifeng was the world's biggest city, with a million people.

NEEDLES AND... CUPS?

For thousands of years, the Chinese have been jabbing, scalding and pummelling each other – for the sake of their health. Having needles stuck into your skin or hot cups placed on your back might look uncomfortable, but doctors and patients alike swear that such treatments not only banish aches and illnesses but also improve your overall sense of wellbeing. So, step this way please…

Yin yang symbol

Life lines

How's your *qi*? The Chinese believe we all have a life force, *qi*, that flows around the body along channels, or meridians. If these channels are blocked, the balance of opposing forces in the body – what the Chinese call *yin* and *yang* – is upset, and illness is the result.

A prickly character

This guy must have been really sick! Actually, it was a stunt to promote the use of acupuncture, at the start of the 2008 Beijing Olympic Games.

DID I REALLY NEED ONE IN MY GUM?

On target

Unblocking channels most often involves acupuncture – inserting long, thin needles into particular points along your meridians known as pressure points or *men* gates. Just relax, you won't feel a thing!

> AT LEAST THIS WAY YOU DON'T INHALE.

> I FEEL GREAT!

ight my fire

cupuncture not having the esired effect? Then you might y moxibustion – attaching urning leaves to the needles heat them. Or ear candling – icking lighted candles in your ars to draw out toxins.

> DO YOU SMELL BURNING?

Press here
Vigorous massage can also help stimulate the meridians.

HOT CUPS

Another option is cupping. Air inside a glass or bamboo cup is warmed. Then when the cup is placed on the skin the air contracts, sucking up the flesh and forming a tight seal. It's said to improve blood flow. It can certainly leave you with some interesting skin patterns!

WANT MORE?

Brush up on the basics ✶ www.tcmworld.org/what_is_tcm

NOW YOU SEE IT...

Running right the way across China, it is, most definitely, the biggest human-made structure on Earth. But no one knows exactly how great the Great Wall of China really is. For it's not just one wall but many. Some date from as early as the 3rd century BC, while others were built in medieval times. And some run unbroken over vast distances, while others branch to dead ends, vanish under water or sand, or peter out in heaps of rubble.

Keep out!
China's first emperor, Qin Shihuang, created the Great Wall in the 3rd century BC to keep out warmongering nomads from the north. The Qin wall was made mainly of rammed earth and rocks and only small sections remain.

Bricks and mortar
From the late 1300s onwards, the Ming rulers rebuilt and extended the wall using bricks and mortar. Long sections of this wall still stretch across fields and rollercoaster along ridges.

Wall of death
Qin Shihuang forced hundreds of thousands of people to work on the wall – up to one-fifth of the population – and thousands of them died on the job. In fact, so many people perished building the wall that it is sometimes called 'the longest cemetery in the world'.

> I'M JUST ANOTHER BRICK IN THE WALL!

Building the wall may have cost the lives of up to two million people.

GLAD TO BE OF SERVICE!

A woof of smoke
As many as 10,000 watchtowers line the Great Wall. Soldiers used to burn huge piles of wolf dung and straw to send signals from one tower to the next.

Getting carried away
Over the centuries parts of the Great Wall have fallen into disrepair or even been carted away to build houses, shops and roads.

Surprise! New sections of the Great Wall are regularly being found, usually in remote forest or desert.

...NOW YOU DON'T

A longstanding myth claims that the Great Wall is the only human-made structure visible from the Moon. However, the first moonwalkers said they couldn't see it. Nor could China's first astronaut, Yang Liwei, despite orbiting Earth 14 times in October 2003.

WALL? WHAT WALL?

WANT MORE?

The wall's length is at least the distance from San Francisco to New York and back.

IN CHARACTER

You might think it's tricky to master handwriting and spelling in English, but you only have 26 letters to deal with. Spare a thought for Chinese kids. Their language is made up of highly complicated symbols or characters, many thousands of which have to be learned before they can write well or read a book. No wonder some people call it the Great Wall of Chinese!

Far sighted
Legend has it that Chinese characters were invented around 2650 BC by the historian Cangjie. Looking at animal tracks in the sand, he realised that things could be represented by signs scratched into a surface. Cangjie was said to have four eyes, so perhaps it's not surprising he spotted this first!

Start simple
The first Chinese characters were probably pictographs – simple representations of the things they referred to.

Sun

Moon

Rain

Mountain

Fish

Cloud

There are now around 80,0000 Chinese characters, though many are seldom used.

Getting abstract
Gradually, combinations of pictographs came to stand for more abstract notions. For example, the characters for woman and child together make 'good', *hao*.

Good =

好

Woman + child

From scratch
In 1899, a herbalist was grinding up bones to make medicine, when he spotted som symbols. It turned out the bone was 3000 years old and carried the oldest Chinese writing ever found. Oops!

Hard graft

All you can do is practise, practise, practise – there are no shortcuts. By age nine, you need to know about 2000 characters. Think you could handle it?

MIND YOUR LANGUAGE!

The characters make learning Chinese hard enough, but for foreigners sounds are an even bigger challenge. Different pronunciations, or tones, can change the meaning of a word entirely. For example, saying *qing wen* one way means 'May I ask something?' But change the tone a fraction and it means 'May I have a kiss?'

WANT MORE?

Learn some basic phrases ✫ **www.standardmandarin.com/chinesephrases**

THE CHAIRMAN'S REVOLUTION

You'll see his face everywhere, watching from posters on buildings and adorning everything from stamps to bank notes. He's Mao Zedong, founder and first chairman of the People's Republic, and he's the man who transformed China. Not only did he introduce Communism, expand industry and modernise agriculture, but he also fearlessly went head to head with the true enemy of the people: the sparrow.

TIMELINE

Mao cap

1912 Fall of the last emperor

1921 Founding of Chinese Communist Party

1927 Civil war breaks out between Nationalis and Communists

1937 Nationalists and Communists unite to fight Japan

1945 Civil war resumes

1949 Founding of People's Republic of China

1958 Mao launches Great Leap Forward

1966 Mao starts Cultural Revolution

1976 Death of Mao

The big winner

From the 1920s, two forces fought for control of China: the Communists under Mao and the Nationalists. In 1949, Mao won out and proclaimed the People's Republic of China.

Public Enemy No

CAREFUL, HE'S A BIG ONE!

WHERE?

Threat to the state

Determined to modernise China, Mao began the so-called Great Leap Forward. He insisted people start industries. He also told them they must get rid of sparrows, as they were eating China's grain. So people blasted, trapped and poisoned those pesky little birds.

GOOD, NO SPARROWS ANYWHERE. BUT WHAT'S THAT BUZZING SOUND?

Out with old ideas

Having dealt with sparrows, Mao moved on to teachers and other insufficiently revolutionary clever-clogs. He sent them to farms to learn how to work with their hands. This was called the Cultural Revolution. Not a good time to wear glasses.

DOWN WITH TEACHERS!

aiting in the wings

t with every sparrow gone, locusts – hich are usually eaten by sparrows – had field day. They chomped through crops, ding hugely to the woes of farmers ring a devastating famine in 1958–61.

More than a billion copies of Mao's Little Red Book have been printed.

UP CLOSE AND PERSONAL

Mao died in 1976, but you can still say hello to him. His embalmed body is displayed in a tomb in Tiananmen Square in Beijing.

Little red thoughts

You can also read his thoughts in his famous Little Red Book. It's essential reading for revolutionaries. No mention of those sparrows, though.

WANT MORE?

Mao never brushed his teeth, preferring to clean them with tea leaves.

TWO WHEELS TO GO

Across China, car ownership is on the rise and city streets are steadily filling with fume-belching, gas-guzzling vehicles. But, as they have done for decades, the vast majority of Chinese still depend on a much humbler and more eco-friendly form of transport, the bicycle.

ON YOUR BIKES, GET SET...GO!

Turning point
The bicycle took off in the 1950s when the Communist Party decided it was the ideal 'people's vehicle'. The main bike of that era, the Flying Pigeon, is the most popular vehicle in history, with more than 500 million sold.

Two-thirds of the world's bikes are made in China, including 9 out of 10 sold in the United States.

NOW, LET'S SEE: IT WAS GREY, WITH TWO WHEELS...

Crazy foreigners
When Westerners first brought bicycles to China in the late 1800s, the locals thought they were mad. Wealthy Chinese preferred to pay someone to carry them in a sedan chair or rickshaw.

Survival skills
There are still around 500 million bicycles on the roads in China. To ride one in chaotic city traffic, you need nerves of steel – and a good memory!

MORE POWER TO THE PEOPLE

For the many Chinese who can't afford a car, motorised bikes – of all shapes and sizes – are the next best thing.

Live wires
Especially popular are eco-friendly electric bikes. More than 120 million of these now buzz around China's streets.

TURN RIGHT!

THESE NEW SELF-ASSEMBLY KITCHENS LOOK GREAT.

NO, LEFT!

All hands aboard
It's amazing what you – and a few friends – can do on a simple bicycle. Just don't try this in a Beijing bike jam!

Loaded up
Bikes are versatile vehicles. Add another wheel and you can transport almost anything – if you've got the legs for it.

WANT MORE?

About 90 per cent of all the electric bikes in the world are sold in China.

THE SECRET OF SILK

About 4700 years ago, someone, somewhere in China, discovered something truly astonishing: that fibre from the cocoon of a particular moth could be woven into a marvellous material, called (in English) silk. Realising the value of this discovery, the Chinese managed to keep the process secret for thousands of years – much to the fury of Western merchants, envoys and emperors.

I STARTED IT ALL, YOU KNOW!

Silkworm moth

Mum's the word
As demand for silk grew, successive Chinese emperors decreed that anyone revealing the secret of its production to foreigners would be put to death.

Fancy fingerwork
If you wanted to make a robe like this one, you needed nimble fingers and infinite patience. Completing it could take up to eight years and six million stitches.

The ancient Romans adored silk and valued it as highly as gold.

Y A THREAD

st, fancy making some silk? First you'll need silkworms,
e caterpillars of the Chinese silkworm moth.

ANYONE WANT THE LAST LEAF?

HELLO? ANYBODY OUT THERE?

UH-OH!

uck in!
tart by feeding the worms with
ulberry leaves, their favourite
nack. This will help them grow
o 70 times their original size.

Spit it out!
After a month each worm
will form a long fibre with
its saliva and wind it around
itself to make a cocoon.

Time to unwind…
Boil the fully formed cocoons to
soften them and get rid of the
pupae. Then unwind the fibre,
which may be up to 1km (0.6mi)
long. Finally, start weaving!

eating a path
n the 2nd century BC, Chinese
erchants took silk to Europe
nd Western merchants travelled
China along the so-called Silk
oad. Yet still the source of silk
remained a
mystery in
the West.

AZING STUFF. YBE IT GROWS ON TREES?

CRAFTY, EH?!

The secret is out
In the 5th century AD, Roman
emperor Justinian persuaded two
Persian monks living in China to
smuggle silkworms to him inside
hollow walking sticks. From those
few worms, the entire European
silk industry grew.

GLAD TO GET RID OF THAT LOAD. WHO SAID SILK WAS LIGHT?

WANT MORE?

Travel the Silk Road ☆ http://idp.bl.uk/pages/education_students.a4d#3

HERE, HAVE A PANDA!

From the 1950s to the 1980s, any head of state visiting China was likely to go home with a hefty parting gift: a real live giant panda. The panda had come to represent the cute and cuddly face of China, so giving one to a passing president or prime minister seemed a great way to promote the nation. And it worked: in countries that received pandas, people flocked to zoos to see them and they became national celebrities.

No Westerner saw a live panda until 1916, when German explorers purchased a cub in China.

Panda diplomacy
The Chinese practice of gifting pandas to foreign nations dates back hundreds of years, but it reached a peak in the late 20th century.

ZZZ

ER, UM... THANKS!

HOW MUCH CAN A PANDA BEAR?

Dwindling supplies
Handing out pandas seemed a rather rash thing to do given their rarity. By the late 1900s land clearance had confined pandas to tiny pockets of forest in the southwest. Even today there may be fewer than 1600 in the wild, most living in protected reserves.

HOW WILL WE FIT THOSE IN OUR CASES?!

SURPRISE! SURPRISE!

MAYBE HE'D LIKE A CUP OF TEA?

it for tat

1972 the Chinese presented
vo pandas, Ling-Ling and
sing-Hsing, to visiting US
resident Richard Nixon.
ixon gave the pandas
the National Zoo in
ashington and later
ot his own back by
ending the Chinese
vo musk oxen.

HEH. JUST YOU WAIT!

Panda mania
A million people visited Ling-Ling and Hsing-Hsing in
their first year at the National Zoo. Similar 'panda mania'
broke out in Britain when Prime Minister Edward Heath
brought back Chia-Chia and Ching-Ching in 1974.

ATS SHOOTS
ND LEAVES A MESS

hink you'd like a pet panda? Well, think again. It might
ook cute as a baby but a panda can grow to 1.8m (6ft)
all and weigh 160kg (350lb). Quite a handful!

Fussy eater
What's more, a panda requires an endless
supply of bamboo shoots – up to 14kg
(30lb) a day – and will eat almost nothing
else. Oh, and a panda poos constantly, as
often as 40 times a day. Still want one?

WANT MORE?

Learn how to help pandas ☆ http://pandasinternational.org

IF YOU CAN'T STAND THE HEAT...

At the height of summer, the average temperature in Beijing is 33°C (91°F), but it often soars as high as 40°C (104°F).

Located far from the cooling influence of the sea, China's capital, Beijing, swelters in summer heat. Ordinary folks have always had to just wipe their brows and tough it out. But if you were an emperor you'd find ways to stay cool. Even if it meant moving mountains. Or telling a few fibs.

I WISH I COULD WEAR SHORTS!

Needing a change of scene
In 1750 Emperor Qianlong was fed up with baking in Beijing. He longed for shady, forested hillsides and wide, cooling waterways. Nowhere around the capital fitted that description. But was that a problem for an emperor? No way!

Dig it?
Qianlong simply had 10,000 workers spend the next 14 years digging out a huge artificial lake, Kunming Lake, and using the earth to make a small mountain, Longevity Hill. Sorted!

Air conditioning
Once he had his water and hills, Qianlong planted gardens and built airy palaces and pavilions. He called his new hang-out the Garden of Clear Ripples, though it's better known now as the Summer Palace.

> EVERY MUM SHOULD HAVE ONE!

PULLING THE STRINGS

Crafty Cixi was the real power behind the throne from 1856 to 1908, manipulating her husband, Emperor Xianfeng, her son, Emperor Tongzhi, and several successors. When officials visited her husband at the Summer Palace, Cixi would whisper instructions to him from behind a screen.

> SHOULD BE GOOD ENOUGH TO FOOL THOSE IMPERIAL BEAN-COUNTERS!

The world's biggest sunshade

So that he and his mum could stroll along the lakeshore while staying out of the sun, Qianlong built a covered walkway, the longest structure of its type in the world, at 728m (2277ft). He also had it decorated with over 8000 exquisite artworks. Such a kind boy!

All aboard the HMS Cixi

In the late 1800s, Empress Cixi rebuilt the Summer Palace, using money she had requested to set up a naval college. She did at least build a boat. Not that it sails, though: it's made of wood, painted to look like marble.

WANT MORE?

Cixi even had a theatre built, so she could watch opera without leaving the palace.

A HANDSOME RETURN

Two hundred years ago, it didn't have much going for it: a small, remote island, home to a few fisherfolk and occasionally raided by pirates. But Hong Kong was still a handy hideout for British merchants. After acquiring a 99-year lease on the island in 1898, the British turned it into one of the world's great trading centres. And when the lease was up, China was only too happy to take Hong Kong back.

S'ALL RIGHT FOR PILLAGING, BUT YOU WOULDN'T WANT TO LIVE THERE!

Location, location, location!

Situated off the south coast of China, Hong Kong Island had no fresh water or farmland. But it did have a sheltered harbour and lay on the major trade route between the Far East and Europe.

THE CHEEK OF IT: NOT WANTING OUR BUSINESS!

CAN WE COME IN?

Getting their way

The sly Brits were smuggling a drug called opium. When China tried to stop this in the mid-1800s, Britain went to war, twice, in the so-called Opium Wars. Victorious both times, Britain forced China to buy its unhealthy merchandise and hand over more territory.

City of refuge

With trade guaranteed, business boomed. At the same time, Hong Kong became a refuge for people fleeing wars and persecution. By 1861, the were 120,000 people livin there; by 1941, 1.6 millio

Rising fast

After World War II, British companies built factories to take advantage of the large workforce, and banks set up shop to supply the funds. Profits soared, high-rises rose higher and the population climbed to seven million by 2009.

> THAT'S THE BEST INVESTMENT WE EVER MADE!

> IT'S THE GREAT CHINESE TAKEAWAY.

> Hong Kong is one of the world's most densely populated places.

Hand it back!

By the time Prince Charles officially handed Hong Kong back to Chinese President Jiang Zemin in 1997, it was a business centre to rival London or New York. China got its island back – and then some!

> WHAT'S THE CHINESE FOR TIGGER?

WHERE EAST MEETS WEST

Not surprisingly, Hong Kong remains an island of Western influence. It's still home to large numbers of foreign people and businesses. It even has China's first Disneyland – and you don't get much more Western than that!

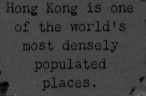

WANT MORE?

Find out what to do in Hong Kong ☆ www.discoverhongkong.com

HONG'S NOT-SO-HEAVENLY KINGDOM

Can you name the deadliest war of all time? World War II is right. And the second worst? No, not World War I but, many say, the Taiping Rebellion. Never heard of it? You're not alone. For this mid-1800s peasant uprising, led by a crazed visionary determined to found a heavenly kingdom on Earth is not widely known – even though it left many millions dead and devastated China.

YEAH, REALLY, HE'S MY BRO'.

Come again?
It all started with an unsuccessful student, Hong Xiuquan. After encounters with Christian missionaries and a series of visions, he claimed he was the second son of god – Jesus's kid brother!

I'LL DO ANYTHING FOR A LOAF OF BREAD!

Whatever you say!
Hong set out to create a 'heavenly kingdom of great peace' (*taiping tianguo* in Chinese) and began recruiting followers. These were tough times of famine and harsh rule by the Qing emperor. Desperate people were ready to believe anything.

WAR BY NUMBERS

The numbers in this grisly scoreboard of the worst wars and their dead are hotly debated, but there's no doubt China has had a rough ride:

- World War II, 1939–45: 40–70 million dead
- Taiping Rebellion, China, 1851–64: 20–50 million dead
- An Lushan Rebellion, China, AD 755–763: 13–35 million dead
- Qing conquest, China, 1616–62: 25 million dead
- World War I, 1914–19: 15 million dead

Out of control

Hong assembled an army that won victory after victory over the Qing forces. By 1853, this 'Taiping' army numbered half a million and had seized the city of Nanjing. Soon the war spread all over China.

Losing it

In Nanjing, Hong proclaimed his 'Taiping Heavenly Kingdom'. But he soon lost his mind completely and locked himself away with his wives, leaving much of the running of the kingdom to his 13-year-old son. What a job!

I LIKE TO BLEND IN.

No surrender

The Qing recruited renowned British officer Charles 'Chinese' Gordon, and his 'Ever-Victorious Army' helped drive the last Taiping back to Nanjing. There in 1864, Hong died and many thousands of Taiping committed suicide rather than surrender.

WANT MORE?

Read the story in detail ☆ www.taipingrebellion.com

NEVER MESS WITH A MONK

As they meditate silently, chant softly or tend their gardens, the Shaolin monks of Mount Shaoshi near Luoyang might appear meek, shy and retiring. But breach their peace or upset their harmonious order and you might suddenly find yourself spinning through the air on your way to a rather uncomfortable meeting with a stone pillar or temple floor. For the Shaolins are the legendary masters of Chinese martial arts, or kung fu.

Fight club

In the 7th century, the monks honed their fighting prowess to defend themselves against bandits. Early techniques involve the use of weapons, but by the 17th century the monks had developed a form of fighting using only their bare hands.

TOO MUCH SITTING AROUND. YOU BOYS NEED SOME EXERCISE!

Bodhidharma

Home of the brave

The Shaolin Monastery was founded in AD 495. It's said that in the 6th century the founder of Zen Buddhism, Bodhidharma, taught the monks a set of exercises which became Shaolinquan, the first martial art.

> I'M JUST PRAYING I CAN GET OUT OF THIS POSITION.

Hard men

Monks rise every day at 5 am to begin study and training. Many exercises focus on toughening the body to turn it into what the monks call an 'iron shirt'.

Get knotted

Shaolin trainees quickly learn a host of handy skills, including headsprings, punching holes in trees with their fingers, running up walls and meditating in very tight spaces.

There are now more than 60 martial arts training schools beside the Shaolin Monastery.

> KUNG FU? I CAN DO THAT STANDING ON MY HEAD.

KUNG FU FIGHTING

In Chinese the term *kung fu* simply means 'skill' and is used to refer to all arts. As well as Shaolinquan, the many forms of martial or fighting arts include:

- Eagle Claw, which specialises in gripping techniques
- Bajiquan, famous for its elbow strikes
- Changquan, noted for its spectacular acrobatic kicks
- Wing Chun, a southern form of close-range combat

Health kicks

Tai chi is a martial art that is widely practised as a form of exercise.

Mini master

In the *Kung Fu Panda* movies, the character of Master Shifu is based on a Shaolin teacher.

WANT MORE?

The media-savvy Shaolin monks have a website ☆ www.shaolin.org.cn/EN

HE WROTE THE RULES

You'd hardly think that some thoughts bandied about 2500 years ago by a poor wandering scholar almost no one wanted to employ would be much heeded in the modern world. But to a quite amazing extent, the ideas of ancient philosopher Confucius still guide how many Chinese live and conduct themselves today – at home, at work and at school.

Say no to violence
Confucius was born in 551 BC, during the so-called Warring States era. Horrified by the violence, he urged people to turn to the idea of *ren*, meaning 'kindness'. But those warring warlords just didn't want to know.

Be loyal to your leader
Confucius died in poverty in 479 BC, but his followers collected his thoughts in a book called the *Analects*. One of its central ideas was that of loyalty – to your country and its ruler. Emperors quite liked that idea and started to listen up.

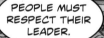

Study hard and you'll succeed
A Confucian idea that caught on big tim was that government jobs should be open to all and awarded on the basis of exams. The Imperial Examinations systen lasted from the 7th to the 20th century and convinced countless generations that studying is A Good Thing. Got that?

Learn the rules
Even today, young children are taught to recite the writings of Confucius. Sometimes very loudly.

Chinese children still study hard, spending an average of nine hours a day at school.

WE'RE RIGHT BEHIND YOU...

Obey your parents
Almost as important as loyalty to a ruler, for Confucius, was respect for ancestors and family. Most modern Chinese still listen carefully to their parents and grandparents, and few will dare miss a family occasion.

RESPECT WISDOM!

No doubt Confucius would be delighted by the respect shown for his ideas in modern China. People flock to his family estate at Qufu, now the site of the Confucius Temple. Not that he ever lived there: the grand estate was set up by his descendants, the Kongs, after successive emperors rewarded them with wealth and titles.

WANT MORE?

Bone up on Confucius's thoughts ✵ www.confucius.org

AN ILL WIND

Spring: it's a word that conjures up images of flowers, blue skies and lambs gambolling across lush green fields. But don't count on such idyllic conditions in China. For spring is when winds whip western desert sands high into the sky and eastwards across the entire country, turning the air into a suffocating smog and coating every surface with a thick layer of orange dust.

Country wide
The sandstorm in this satellite photo is whirling over almost the whole of China. Imagine how many people are under that!

The sky is falling
Once the winds are strong enough, the sand starts flying. This storm is about to engulf the northwestern city of Golmud.

Storms dump over one million tonnes of sand on Beijing every year.

arch of the dunes

ndstorms have got worse recently due to
esertification – land turning into desert as a
sult of temperature rises and the clearing of
es. Windblown sand
nes are advancing
st and are now just
km (50mi) from
ijing. Within 20
ars they could
gulf the capital.

> **WHAT'S WRONG WITH A LITTLE BIT OF SAND?**

Toxic cocktail

Airborne sand combines with China's
high levels of industrial pollution to
create a dangerous mix of sand and toxic
substances such as carbon monoxide,
arsenic, lead, coal ash and pesticides. Yuck!

China's dust storms
can trigger heavier
snowfalls in the
western United
States – a bonus for
skiers at least!

> **HE'S NORMALLY VERY CHATTY.**

l a bit hazy

e dust regularly shrouds the
ajor cities of the east, swirling
rough streets and reducing
sibility. Airports often have to
ose and flights are grounded.

Wrapping up

People have learned to cope with
the dust. They stay at home or
wear masks and old clothes.

WANT MORE?

Up to a quarter of Los Angeles' smog is thought to come from China.

THE OLDEST SHOW IN TOWN

It's an amazing spectacle: colourful, beautiful, magical. And, yes, it's a bit baffling. A 200-year-old form of theatre, Chinese opera combines music, dance, martial arts, bizarre costumes and a lot of weird make-up. But don't let that put you off. It's not to be missed, and there are ways to work out what's going on!

Listen up!
The music is played by a small orchestra of stringed, wind and percussion instruments. Pay attention to the percussion, which often alerts you to dramatic moments.

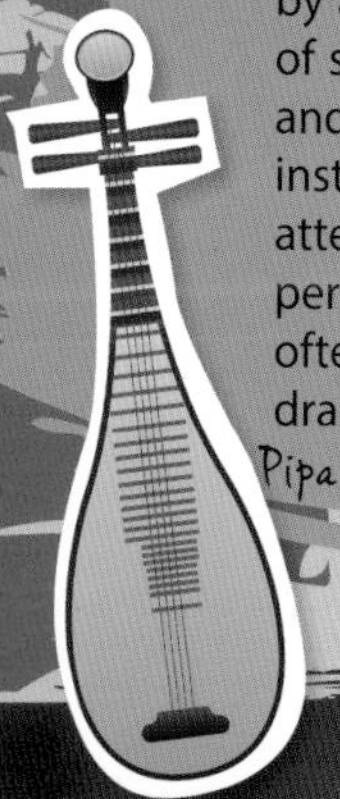

Pipa

IT'S A TRULY UPLIFTING EXPERIENCE!

WE ALL NEED A LEG-UP NOW AND AGAIN!

Performance booster
Sure, it's performed in Chinese, but often it's a local dialect so many of the Chinese don't understand it all either. That means translations are often displayed above the stage – sometimes in English too. How helpful is that?

REMEMBER: DAN IS NOT A MAN!

The famous four

There are really only four main roles (from left to right): Dan, the female lead; Sheng, the male lead; Jing, the supporting male; and Chou, the clown. All are usually recognisable.

Colour code

Look closely at the actors' make-up and masks and remember: red stands for loyalty and courage; blue and green are worn by brave, hot-headed characters; yellow and white indicate shifty types; and black stands for wisdom and strength. Got it?

Check out the moves

Watch out for acrobatic moves and fiery tricks. These are always appreciated by the audience. Soon you'll be nodding approvingly too!

READ THE SIGNS

Stay alert and you'll see that some actions are represented by gestures. Waving a whip stands in for riding a horse, for example. Patting the cheeks tells you a character is crying. Stroking a beard means a character is thinking.

WANT MORE?

History at ☆ http://asianhistory.about.com/od/arthistoryinasia/a/BeijingOpera.htm

ONE BIG BUDDHA

What has ears as tall as a two-storey house and toes the size of a small car? No, not a prehistoric elephant but Dà Fó, the Grand Buddha of Leshan, in Sichuan, central China. Standing a whopping 71m (230ft) tall, it's the biggest stone Buddha in the world!

> DON'T YOU DARE TICKLE MY FEET!

In one ear
Those long-lobed ears are 7m (23ft) high. The earhole looks like a top spot for a bird's nest!

The great protector
Dà Fó stands where three rivers merge, creating dangerous currents. The statue was started in AD 713 by a monk called Haitong, who believed it would protect river travellers.

Top to toe
While working on the excavation, Haitong lived in a cave behind Dà Fó's head. After he died, teams of monks and craftsmen slaved for 90 years to complete the carving.

> I WONDER IF HIS PARENTS WERE TALL.

Before *After*

ON A GRAND SCALE

Soon after Buddhism reached China in the 1st century AD, monks began creating extraordinary giant images of their religion's founder.

Spruced up

Just like you, Dà Fó needs a good scrub now and again. In his case it's not just to make him presentable but also to prevent erosion of the stone.

> I'VE SAID TO HIM, YOU CAN'T JUST SLEEP ALL DAY...

Dà Fó's hair incorporates 1021 coiled buns, each one a stone peg slotted into the head.

Buddha at rest

At Dazu in southwestern China, a 15m (90ft) Buddha lies on its side behind statues of the men who paid for the shrine's construction.

> OH NO – FORGOT MY PRAYER BOOK!

> WE THINK BIG!

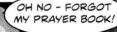

Keep off!

It's said that 100 people could sit in a ring on just one of the giant statue's feet, and at one time they were a popular picnic spot. But nowadays signs warn against treading on Dà Fó's toes!

Up for it?

To reach the 4th-century shrines on Maiji Shan in northwestern China, you have to climb hundreds of rickety wooden stairs attached to the side of a sheer cliff. Those monks must have had a head for heights!

The Longmen Caves at Luoyang contain over 100,000 carvings of the Buddha.

MADE IN CHINA

Take a close look at your toys, computers, music players and sports gear. Chances are you'll find a 'Made in China' label on most of them. For China makes and exports to the rest of the world a staggering range of stuff. It's all down to the country's productive mix of cutting-edge technology, giant factories and the world's biggest workforce.

Ready and willing
China has an almost endless supply of increasingly skilled workers. Not only that, they generally work for much lower pay than workers in the West.

'I'M A YANKIE-DOODLE DANDY...'

Heading your way
All this has resulted in ever greater piles of stuff being shipped from China to almost every corner of the world – including yours!

Ways to save
Low wages, plentiful factories, readily available technology – what's not to like for manufacturers? It's no wonder that many Western firms have been shifting their production to China. It's partly how they keep their prices low.

Millions of American flags are made in China.

It's a shoe-in
China makes almost three-quarters of all shoes sold in the United States – and around 70 per cent of the world's umbrellas.

WELL...IT'S WHERE WE COME FROM!

The toy story
China produces 90 per cent of the world's toys, including at least three-quarters of all those sold in America.

AND THERE'S LOTS MORE ON ITS WAY!

Chips with that?
Half of all notebook computers run on chips made in the city of Chengdu, which is the base for 1400 technology companies.

ANOTHER SIX MILLION? NO PROBLEM!

elling out
ut of 1.8 billion mobile phones made nnually, about 1 billion are made in hina, mostly around the southern city Shenzhen. Six thousand Shenzhen ompanies work in the industry.

ROLL UP, ROLL UP...

Malls are popping up all over China – not that people are always ready for them. Opened in 2005, New South China Mall, in Dongguan, is the world's biggest mall. But due to poor transport services and low local wages it remains almost empty of shops.

WANT MORE?

Factories in the east-coast town of Datang make nine billion socks every year.

GOING WITH THE GRAIN

Rice is the food that turned China upside down. In ancient times, the north was the happening place while the rice-growing south was a swampy backwater with few people. But from the 6th century, rice fields began yielding giant crops. By the 1400s the south was home to three-quarters of all Chinese, and still is. And not only is rice now China's biggest crop, it's the staple food of half the world's people!

Brown rice is simply white rice with its husk still on.

Food for thought
Ever wondered what rice really is? It's the dried seed of the rice plant. Wild rice was first gathered in China 11,000 years ago and rice was first farmed there around 7000 BC.

TIME FOR A BREAK, I THINK.

Quick turnaround
Some varieties of rice grow in just three months. Then all you need to do is drain the field, harvest the crop, separate the seed from the husk – and start over again. Three crops a year is the usual target – phew!

Mud, glorious mud
If you want to roll out a rice crop, you need to get down and dirty. Rice is grown in flooded beds called paddy fields, and bending down to plant the seedlings is back-breaking work.

ONE SLIP AND I'M IN THE SOUP.

Stepping up production
Cut flat terraces into hillsides and you can grow rice on even the steepest slopes. As long as you have good balance and a head for heights!

RECYCLED RICE

The Chinese have found a host of uses for rice. Among other things, it's turned into wine, flour, straw, paper, crackers, noodles and dumplings.

Instead of 'How are you?', Chinese people often greet each other with the phrase 'Have you had your rice today?'

Rice flour was once used as face-whitening make-up. Talk about a pancake face!

ANYONE FOR TABLE TENNIS?

WELL, HAVE YOU?!

Sticky stuff
Early Chinese builders used mashed sticky rice as mortar for walls – including the Great Wall of China!

Rice dumplings

WANT MORE?

Rice around the world ☆ www.fao.org/rice2004/en/aboutrice.htm

A LITTLE CORNER OF...WHEREVER

After the Treaty of Nanjing of 1842 allowed foreigners to live in some Chinese cities for the first time, Shanghai, the east coast's major port, quickly became home to thousands of people from all over the world. Through the early 1900s, wealthy foreign settlers built grand recreations of the streets and buildings of their homelands – Britain, France, America, Russia and more. Soon you could hardly tell *where* you were!

The Bund

The Paris of the East
Pavement cafes, croissants, chic boutiques – surely it's Paris? No, it's the French Concession, formerly home to Shanghai's French community and still one of its most glamorous neighbourhoods.

French Concession

JUST LIKE 'OME!

GOSH, I DIDN'T KNOW HORSES PLAYED CRICKET!

Gathering place
Europeans liked to meet to watch horse races at the city's Ol[d] Racecourse, which a[lso] had a cricket pitch.

Rule Britannia

Remove a few signs and it could almost be London. The riverfront Bund is still lined with British colonial-style buildings, built in the 1920s when Shanghai was the world's third largest financial centre.

Nanking Road

ALL IT NEEDS IS A LITTLE RAIN AND FOG...

The New York of the West

By the 1920s Shanghai had a wild, colourful nightlife that rivalled that of Jazz-Age New York. Oversized American cars prowled past brightly lit bars, cinemas, nightclubs and dance halls.

In 1932, Shanghai was the world's fifth largest city and home to **70,000** foreigners, or 'Shanghailanders'.

UNDERWORLD

Shanghai had American-style nightlife, and the gangsters to match. Two rival criminal groups, the Green Gang and the Red Gang, had long fought for control of Shanghai's illegal businesses.

I'M ALL EARS, HUANG.

Police assistance

By the 1920s, the Green Gang, led by Du Yuesheng, or 'Big-eared Du', had won out. This was thanks to support from 'Pockmarked Huang', another gangster – who also happened to be a police chief!

WANT MORE?

History, photos, maps and more ☆ www.virtualshanghai.net

HOW COOL IS THAT?

Midwinter in northeastern China. It's −30°C (−22°F) in the city of Harbin – teeth-chatteringly cold. You'd think everyone would be indoors huddled round a fire, or heading south to warmer climes. But no, hordes of people are not only mad enough to be outside but are busy shaping snow and ice to make sculptures and massive scale-model buildings. The entire city is gearing up for what is undoubtedly China's coolest annual show!

Harbin's ice festival began in 1985 and now draws 800,000 visitors every year.

HE COULD REALLY DO WITH A HAT.

Night lights
By day they might be simply shades of white, but by night, thanks to crafty computer-controlled lighting, the ice and snow take on every colour of the rainbow in amazing 'ice-lantern' shows.

Snow show
Snowmen? Pah, that's child's play! At Harbin snow is rolled, piled and shaped with astounding artistry to create huge monuments and astonishingly realistic giant figures. Not a carrot in sight.

The world comes to Harbin

Once you've got the hang of building with ice, the world's your oyster. Knock up another Great Wall of China, an Egyptian Sphinx or a European cathedral? No problem.

Bright spark

Once upon a time an ice lantern was just a hollow bucket-shaped block of ice with a candle inside. Technology has clearly moved on!

On the slide

You have to keep your wits about you climbing all those crystal-clear stairs, but coming down you can take the weight off your feet and just let go!

GLAD I WORE ALL THREE PAIRS OF THERMAL KNICKERS!

BARMY BEARS?

Still not cool enough for you? Then how about joining Harbin's 'polar bears'? These hardy water-lovers take the plunge into a pool hacked out of the frozen Songhua River. Seasoned splashers swear it improves blood circulation and makes them more alert. Well, you're hardly likely to doze off in there!

OH-OH. MY HANDS ARE STUCK FAST.

WANT MORE?

Keep an eye on China's weather ☆ www.weather.com.cn/english

YOU CAN TAKE IT WITH YOU

BETTER GET STARTED. THIS COULD TAKE A WHILE!

In ancient China, death was not the end. People believed you moved on to another life. Not only that but you could even take stuff with you. For ordinary folk that meant a few favourite knicknacks, for nobles usually some fancier treasures. But for Qin Shihuang, First Emperor of China, it meant, literally, his entire world.

Thinking ahead

Qin Shihuang began planning what to take with him as soon he became emperor, in 246 BC And over the next 36 years, he had over 700,000 people build and furnish his tomb.

Taking no chances

Clearly Qin Shihuang suspected the afterlife might not be all peace and tranquillity, as he decided to take along an entire army. Sure, the soldiers were made of clay, or terracotta, but there were 8000 of them. And they had real weapons and chariots.

WE'RE READY FOR ANYTHING!

Qin's world

At the centre of his tomb Qin placed a bronze palace – full size of course. Around it he had labourers dig trenches and fill them with liquid mercury to represent the seas and rivers of the Qin world. And he had the tomb ceiling painted to look like the stars.

...dividual treatment
...stickler for detail, Qin
...ade sure everything
... least looked real.
...ach soldier was given
...fferent clothes and
...cial features.

A HEADS-UP

A farmer digging for
water in a field in 1974
must have got the shock
of his life when he dug
up a lifelike clay head.
That was the find that
led archeologists to Qin's tomb. Yet still
only a small area has been excavated
and most of the site, including the main
palace, awaits discovery.

COOL OUTFIT, HUH?

Some clay soldiers
were armed with
crossbows primed to
shoot anyone who
entered the tomb.

You're coming too!
For company, Qin took along dozens of wives –
they were buried alive near his body. Finally,
Qin's successors rounded up all the craftsmen
who knew the tomb's secrets and walled them
inside too, before covering everything with a
mound of earth 76m (250ft) tall.

QIN'S ARMY

★ 8000 soldiers
★ 130 chariots
★ 670 horses
★ 10,000 weapons

I KNEW THIS JOB
WOULD BE THE DEATH
OF ME!

WANT
MORE?

The entire tomb is thought to cover 50 sq km (20 sq mi).

A BIRD IN THE HAND

Fishing: it can be a bit slow, can't it? Chucking out a line or net and then just sitting there, hoping that a fish will bite the hook or swim into the trap. But crafty Chinese anglers have managed to avoid all that hanging around *and* get something else to do most of the work – a bird. Their method is called cormorant fishing and you might like to give it a go.

Where it's at
To learn from the masters, head south to Guilin, a major centre of cormorant fishing, where spectacular limestone towers line the Li River.

Tie a line
To prevent the cormorant swallowing all but the smallest fish, you have to tie a cord round its neck. That way bigger fish will stay in its throat.

BEST BETS

It's essential that you catch and tame the right kind of bird. In China, it's usually a great cormorant, though sometimes a darter is used; in Japan, the smaller Japanese cormorant is favoured. Tie each line to the right species:

1. Great cormorant
2. Japanese cormorant
3. Rubber duck
4. Darter

Follow the light
Night time is the right time. Use a lamp to attract fish and light the way. Then pop the birds in the water and they'll paddle along beside the boat scooping up fish.

I'M A BIT SICK OF THIS!

THEY'RE ENTIRELY THE WRONG KINDS OF BIRDS, YOU KNOW.

Coming up!
A little bit of squeezing and tickling will persuade a bird to hand over its catch!

THAT'S SEVEN. YOUR TURN TO COUGH UP!

Smart anglers
The Chinese developed this nifty method more than 1000 years ago.

KEEPING COUNT

Studies of cormorants have shown that the birds can actually count. Fishermen usually give them every eighth fish to eat. After they have handed over seven, the birds refuse to move until they are given their reward.

WANT MORE?

The Li River is one of China's most scenic areas ☆ www.visitguilin.org

TASTE TEST

China is a place for adventurous eaters. Not only can you tantalise your tastebuds with a totally scrumptious range of rice and noodle dishes, but you can also try out a host of delicacies and titbits you've almost certainly never sampled before. Feeling peckish – and brave?

AW...SO CUTE!

PEEK-A-BOO!

As fresh as it gets
Seafood has got to be fresh, and live is as fresh as it gets. In China, you can not only select live sea creatures and have them quickly boiled or roasted, you can also eat them while they're still wriggling on your plate – octopus, shrimp, squid, crab and more.

All you can eat
Long experience of famine and poverty has taught the Chinese to make the most of every food source. This means you can sample almost any meat you care (or don't care) to think of, including donkey, yak and dog, as well as a huge range of plant roots, mosses, seaweeds and insect larvae.

Many Chinese consider eating airy foods such as butter and cheese to be quite disgusting.

ON THE MENU

Got a strong stomach? Think you can handle anything? Then take your pick from this menu of regional specialities.

Ducks' tongues

Whole pig face

sticky business

a hurry? Street vendors sell st foods on sticks, including arrows, silkworm chrysalises, cadas, grasshoppers, starfish nd seahorses. Live scorpions e skewered and quickly asted in hot oil – luckily at eliminates their sting!

STARTERS

Snake skin with peppers
Ducks' tongues
Shark's stomach soup
Boiled frog in radish soup
Dog-brain soup

MAIN COURSES

Stir-fried camel foot
Simmered mountain rat with black beans
Whole pig face
Solidified duck blood
Cow's lung in chilli sauce
Spicy frogs' legs
Sliced donkey with noodles

DESSERTS

Insect cake
Red bean ice cream

Spit in your soup

Tiny swallow nests that the birds make with their saliva are considered a great delicacy in China. They are usually dished up as a soup, with the nest floating in broth.

WANT MORE?

Learn how to cook and eat Chinese food ☆ http://chinesefood.about.com

WHEN CHINA WENT TO SEA

Great sea voyages shaped our world – think of Columbus reaching the Americas – and they created global empires for nations such as Britain, Spain and Portugal. China, though, could have beaten them all to it. In the early 1400s it had the world's biggest fleet of ships, which undertook several incredible journeys. Had those voyages continued, the world might be a very different place.

Travelling in style
Yongle had more than 1600 ships kitted out for Zheng He's voyages. And not just any old ships, but the biggest ones ever built.

Zheng He

COMING SOON, TO A PORT NEAR YOU!

Go west young man!
In 1405, Ming emperor Yongle commissioned Admiral Zheng He to lead the first of what would be seven voyages across the Indian Ocean to the West.

WHICH WAY IS UP?

The Chinese really got their bearings on the sea front by inventing the magnetic compass, which was first used during the 11th century.

SO, ARE WE AT THE SHARP END?

Just add water
The earliest compasses consisted of a magnetised needle floating in water.

Portuguese caravel

Chinese treasure ship

AHOY THERE, MAKE WAY!

DID YOU HEAR SOMETHING?

Call that a ship!
The fleet's flagships, the treasure ships, were between 120 and 150m (400 and 500ft) long – vastly bigger than a Portuguese ship of the period.

IT'S NICE TO SEE A BIT OF THE WORLD!

Zheng He's first fleet consisted of 317 ships, with a crew of 27,000 – including doctors, naturalists and astrologers.

Well supplied
The treasure ships carried trade goods such as silk and porcelain, and massive supplies of food – they even grew vegetables on board! Souvenirs gathered by the fleet included a giraffe – the first to reach China.

Seen enough?
Over seven journeys, the fleet visited India, Arabia and Africa. But then Yongle died. His successors decided the voyages were a waste of money, and cancelled further trips. China then turned inwards once more.

WANT MORE?

Some think Zheng He also reached the Americas, but this remains unproven.

GODS AND MONSTERS

China's beginnings are a blur of history, religious beliefs and fantastical legends. Powerful gods are said to have created the world, and the Chinese kingdom. Though the forces of darkness have often threatened to destroy these works, great heroes have usually been at hand to save the day.

YOU'D NEVER THINK CLOUDS WOULD BE SO HEAVY!

Giving his all

Some say it all started with Pangu, a huge hairy guy with two horns. He held up the sky for 18,000 years to separate it from the Earth. When he died, his eyes became the Sun and Moon, his hair the trees, his blood the rivers. Fleas on his body turned into animals and humans.

SORRY, FOLKS!

Top god

Others believe the world was begun by a group of gods led by the Jade Emperor. He is said to have made humans out of clay but then left them out in the rain, which is why we have disabilities and sicknesses. D'oh!

Demon

Devil

What a guy!

Legend has it that China was founded by the Yellow Emperor, Huangdi, who also introduced houses, carts, boats and writing and defeated the six-armed, four-eyed tyrant Chi You. These amazing feats are still celebrated on 4 April each year.

ALTOGETHER NOW: 'FOR HE'S A JOLLY GOOD FELLOW…'

ROOM FOR ONE MORE? AND A DONKEY?

Super powers

The Eight Immortals are a group of legendary figures with super powers, who are said to fight evil, help people in distress and restore peace. Some Chinese still worship them, and they have even featured in an X-Men comic book. Now that's immortality!

In 2006, DC Comics introduced a group of superheroes called The Great Ten, based on figures from Chinese myths.

Shape shifter

One of the most popular Chinese heroes is the Monkey King, Sun Wukong. Amazingly strong, he carries a staff that weighs 8100kg (18,000lb), can somersault 54,000km (33,500mi) and can transform himself into 72 different creatures.

READY FOR SOME MONKEY BUSINESS?

Jet Li as the Monkey King, in the movie Forbidden Kingdom

WANT MORE?

Monkey King comic strip ☆ www.china-on-site.com/monkey.php

LONG WAY TO THE TOP

One of the highest cities in the world, the ancient Tibetan capital of Lhasa, in western China, is a long way from anywhere. Travelling by road from Beijing takes several days via hair-raising mountain tracks and even China's speedy modern trains need three days to arrive. But if you're a devout Tibetan Buddhist, you'll be happy to take the hard way to this holy city – and walk.

An early start
Most Tibetan Buddhists plan to make the pilgrimage to Lhasa at some point, and some get a head start. Kids as young as five set off, sometimes leaving their parents for years and walking with other relatives.

Portable prayer wheel

Into thin air
Heading west, pilgrims climb into Tibet's high, cold, barren plateau. The air is so thin, it's hard to breathe. But at least the slow route allows you to acclimatise!

I'M TEMPTED TO JUST STAY HERE A WHILE.

Even harder yards
Trekking is tough enough, but if you're really serious you don't just walk. Every three steps you lie full out on the ground – an additional form of devotion called kowtowing.

NOW THIS IS FUN!

The end in sight

After such an epic trek, the sight of Lhasa could be overwhelming! Dominating the city is Potala Palace, the former home of Tibetan religious leader the Dalai Lama.

AT LAST!

Spinning around
In Lhasa, pilgrims walk twice-daily circuits of the holiest site, Jokhang Temple, turning prayer wheels – cylinders bearing religious texts.

Potala Palace has 1000 rooms and houses 10,000 shrines and more than 200,000 holy statues.

I CHURN IT OUT!

HIGHER, HIGHER!

Some Buddhists take their devotion even further – and higher. Rongbuk Monastery is the highest monastery in the world and lies within sight of Mount Everest.

Buttering up
Pilgrims provide yak butter to keep holy candles alight.

Paying respects
And they make offerings, filling entire rooms with money.

WANT MORE?

Tibet is the world's highest place, with an average elevation of 4900m (16,000ft).

BALANCING ACTS

Can you ride a unicycle? Juggle? Balance a tray of drinks on a stick on the end of your nose? And can you do all those things at the same time? Yes? Great! Then you could sign up for one of China's many acrobat schools. That's as long as you're still under eight years old and ready for ten years of gruelling training. Sound okay?

Are you flexible?
The first thing you'll do at acrobat school is get your body into shape. Or rather, many really odd shapes. You might need a helping hand.

ONCE THOSE LEGS POINT STRAIGHT UP, YOU'LL BE READY TO MOVE ON.

UP THERE WITH THE BEST

When you make it as a Chinese acrobat, you becom part of a prestigious traditio that stretches back 2000 years. Acrobats have been revered since the Han Dynas (206 BC–AD 220) and often performed for emperors. You family will be so proud!

Pick a trick
Maybe your speciality will be a brilliant balancing trick like this one. Just don't practise with your mum's best glassware.

Keep it up!
It's essential you learn to juggle just about anything – balls, sticks, plates, even tables. And not just with your hands. That would be too easy.

THE DRINKS ARE ON ME!

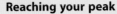

WE'RE REALLY OOKED ON THIS NOW!

Reaching your peak
Eventually, if all goes well (and there are no serious injuries), you might get to tour the world with a professional troupe, enjoying the excitement, the applause and the lime light.

IN THE LINE-UP

Acrobatic performances are also known as Chinese variety art. Your repertoire will usually include the following:

☆ Conjuring ☆
☆ Contortionism ☆
☆ Plate spinning ☆
☆ Balancing glasses ☆
☆ Tightrope walking ☆
☆ Tumbling ☆
☆ Lion dance ☆
☆ Pole balancing ☆
☆ Hoop diving ☆
☆ Cycle tricks ☆
☆ Juggling ☆

WANT MORE?

China has about 120 acrobatic troupes and more than 12,000 performers.

A DROWNED WORLD

What if you had to move because the government wanted to build something where your home is? And not just you, but your whole village, town or city. Hard to imagine, isn't it? But that's exactly what has happened to more than one million people living along central China's Yangtze River.

HOME, SWEET HOME!

Gorgeside living
The people were living along the Three Gorges. It's one of China's most scenic areas, so they probably thought they had it pretty good.

Water power
In 1994, the government started building a giant dam on the river, to harness its swift-flowing waters for power generation and prevent flooding downstream.

NO WAY AM I LEAVING IT BEHIND!

Moving on...or under
The dam raised the river level in the gorges by 100m (330ft). About 1.4 million people had to shift to new housing on higher ground – or start swimming!

YOU SHOULD SEE WHAT'S DOWN THERE!

Altogether the dam's waters have drowned:
13 cities, **140** towns, **1350** villages and **1300** archeological sites

A watery grave?
Early people of the Yangtze placed their dead in coffins and perched them on sheer cliffs. Due to the raised river level, some now lie beneath the waters – while others can be viewed at closer quarters.

HEY, I CAN SEE MY HOUSE FROM HERE!

Window on the past
Hundreds of historic sites were swamped, including ancient stone carvings at Baiheliang. An underwater viewing room was built so people can still see them.

POWERING UP

Completed in 2006, the dam is not only one of the world's largest dams but also the biggest power-producing unit ever built. It will supply at least 3 per cent of China's electricity and protect 15 million people from flooding.

Turbines inside the dam

WANT MORE?

Dams are constantly being built in China – the country has 86,000 already!

WHAT I DID ON MY HOLIDAYS

Venice, Italy, 1271, and he's 17 years old. His dad asks if he fancies going on a business trip. Shouldn't take too long, says Dad. But somehow just getting there takes four *years*. And then they meet this old Khan guy and the next thing you know young Marco Polo is running all over his empire, for 17 years! Back home, Marco tells the story of his trip and – whaddya know? – it's a bestseller! And now it's all China, China, China!

ARE YOU SURE EAST IS THIS WAY?

Dad had a plan
Marco Polo's dad, Niccolò, and uncle, Maffeo, were successful merchants from Venice who had made one trip China. It looked like they could do a roaring trade there, so they decided go back – and took Marco with them

We saw amazing things
On the way to China, wars and bandits made the Polos take many detours, and illnesses led to long stopovers. In 1275 they arrived at last and met Emperor Kublai Khan. They were astonished by his sumptuous palaces.

GO AND TELL THEM THEY HAVE TO PAY MORE TAXES? ER, OKAY!

HOW ABOUT SOME PARMESAN? IT'S ALL THE RAGE IN ITALY!

I went on a side trip
Kublai Khan made Marco a special ambassador and sent him to different parts of his empire.

MARCO? HE'S MY MAIN MAN!

Marco's book inspired Columbus to seek a way to China – by going west across the Atlantic.

Then I wrote it down
The Polos got home in 1295 – just in time for a war between Venice and Genoa. Jailed by the Genoese, Marco recounted his trip to cellmate and writer Rustichello da Pisa.

IT WAS SUNNY ...AND NICE.

HM, LET'S LIVEN IT UP A BIT, SHALL WE?

They can't get enough of it!
Published around 1300, Marco's book, *Il Milione*, was a sensation. It sent traders scurrying east, had people clamouring for Chinese goods such as spices and porcelain, and made people eager to learn more about the mysterious East.

Chinese porcelain

BUT DID HE REALLY GO?

Some people think Marco made it all up. He didn't mention tea or the Great Wall, and he said there were dog-faced people living in India. But most historians believe the account is true, just slightly eccentric!

DID YOU SEE THE CRAZY OUTFIT THAT ITALIAN GUY WAS WEARING?

TOTALLY WEIRD, MAN!

WANT MORE?

The Polos covered more than 24,000km (15,000mi) on their travels.

THE WRITE STUFF

Can you imagine your handwriting being framed and hung in a gallery? In China, the art of handwriting, or calligraphy, is universally appreciated and admired. A few deft strokes of a paintbrush can provoke nods of approval, gasps of amazement and sighs of wonder. And a single written word or character might take pride of place in a museum or be sold for a fortune.

Forever *yong*
The eight basic strokes of calligraphy are all combined in the Chinese character *yong*, meaning 'forever'. Within any character, the eight strokes must be painted in a set order.

THE FOUR TREASURES

A traditional calligrapher works with paper, brush, ink stick and ink stone. Together these tools are known as the Four Treasures of the Scholar.

Inky black
Made from soot and resin, the ink stick must be rubbed in water on an ink stone to create the ink.

HEY YOU, GET OFF MY ART!

Physical graffiti
Employing water instead of ink and paving stones in place of paper, artists regularly hold calligraphy competitions in Chinese parks. This pastime is also seen as a good way to keep fit.

SAME OLD SAME OLD!

So many ways to say…
This collector is displaying a set of 10,000 different handpainted characters, all representing the word 'longevity' or 'long life'.

The art of calligraphy dates back at least 4000 years.

THE PRICE IS RIGHT!

Highly prized
One of the most famous and revered calligraphers in history is Wang Xizhi, who lived during the 4th century. None of his original works survive, but copies do. In 2011 a medieval copy of one of his scrolls, consisting of just four lines of writing, sold for US$46 million!

I GOT TOP MARKS.

STOP RABBITING ON ABOUT IT!

Practice makes…clothes
Young children practise calligraphy from an early age. These school kids have created wacky costumes based on the character for 'rabbit', to mark the Chinese Year of the Rabbit.

WANT MORE?
View masterworks ✶ www.chinaonlinemuseum.com/calligraphy-masters.php

CUTTING A DASH

Throughout history, China's rulers have set benchmarks for style with their swanky outfits and outlandish accessories. But although you might admire their sumptuous silks, groovy headgear and wacky hairstyles, there are some Chinese fashions you'll be glad you missed out on.

> AS LONG AS WE ALL FACE THE SAME WAY, WE'LL BE FINE.

> YOU SHOULD SEE WHAT I'VE GOT UP THE OTHER SLEEVE!

Room to spare
For centuries, the height of fashion was a long silk robe tied at the waist with a belt. Fabulous patterns and rich colours, like those of this Tang-era robe, were a mark of wealth and privilege – as were gigantic sleeves.

Hazardous headwear
From the 2nd century BC, black hats were another status symbol. During the Song Dynasty, officials wore hats with two flaps that extended outwards from the head – a much as 1m (3ft). Imagine the injuries they must have caused!

Making a point
Long fingernails were a sign of wealth, as they indicated that you didn't have to do any work with your hands. This guy must have been loaded!

In the Ming era, women painted two tiny red petals on their lips to make a flower shape.

THE BIG SQUEEZE

From 1100 or so, it became fashionable for women to have really tiny tootsies, known as lotus feet. Getting just the right look involved binding a girl's feet tightly from an early age so that the toes curled under the sole and the arches bent upwards and usually broke. Ouch!

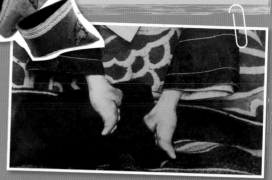

XXXSmall

The unfortunate women had no choice but to get used to tottering on their twisted stumps. Not until the 20th century was foot-binding banned.

> IT'S THIS DYNASTY'S MUST-HAVE LOOK, SIR!

An orderly queue

When the Manchu founded the Qing Dynasty in 1644, they made everyone adopt their rather severe style – or face death! In particular, hair had to be shaved at the front and tied in a long pigtail, or queue, at the back.

> OH DEAR, I'D BETTER CHECK THE CHAIRMAN'S MEASUREMENTS AGAIN!

Big in Beijing

After the 1912 revolution, wealthy women began wearing the elegant *cheongsam* dress. Men adopted the *zhongshan*, a military-style jacket and trousers. Later renamed the Mao suit after style guru Chairman Mao Zedong, it was very practical – as long as you got the right size.

Modern cheongsam dress

WANT MORE?

In the 1800s, roughly half of all Chinese women had bound feet.

FAST TRACK TO THE FUTURE

The face of China is changing at top speed.
Futuristic buildings are rapidly reshaping city skylines in
sci-fi style. Gargantuan railways, bridges and highways
are spanning seas and deserts. And superfast forms
of transport are whisking people here, there and
everywhere, shrinking distances and
bringing the outside world that
big bit closer.

JUST HOPE
THEY'VE FINISHED
THE RUNWAY.

Between 2008
and 2020, China
plans to build 97
new airports!

ARE YOU SURE
WE'RE THE
RIGHT WAY UP?

Reaching for the sky
China now has almost half
of the world's top 20 highest
skyscrapers, including the
Shanghai Financial Centre
(left) and Jin Mao Tower.

Visions realised
Famous architects are being
invited to let their imaginations
run riot and create ultramodern
buildings. Known to locals as
the Bird's Egg, Beijing's National
Centre for the Performing Arts
was dreamed up by French
architect Paul Andreu.

Way to go

While relatively few Chinese (1 in 16) own a car, traffic jams are already a problem – one snarl-up in Beijing in 2010 stretched for 100km (60mi) and took nine days to clear. Imagine what it will be like if China matches the United States, where three out of every four people possess a car!

> UH-OH, DID WE BRING ANY FOOD?

Bridging the gaps

Opened in 2011, the Jiaozhou Bridge is the world's longest over-sea bridge. Extending for 42.5km (26.5mi), it links the cities of Qingdao and Huangdo across Jiaozhou Bay and is designed to withstand earthquakes and typhoons.

SPEEDING UP

China introduced high-speed trains in 2007 and already has by far the world's longest high-speed network. Plans are afoot to connect it to Europe.

> AS SOON AS I PRESS THIS LITTLE BUTTON HERE, YOU'LL BE FLYING TO BEIJING.

> WILL THE TRAIN COME TOO?

Express delivery

Shanghai's Maglev train, which links the city to the airport, can operate at speeds of up to 430km/h (267mph).

City link

The Beijing–Shanghai High-Speed Railway covers the 1318km (819mi) journey between the cities in less than five hours.

WANT MORE?

The Bird's Egg ☆ www.paul-andreu.com/pages/projets_recents_operapek_g.html

GOING OFF WITH A BANG

Imagine their astonishment. In the 9th century, Chinese monks searching for a substance that would grant eternal life whipped up a mix of sulphur, charcoal and potassium nitrate (also called saltpetre). Touching it to a flame they found it not only burned brightly but instantly exploded – with a blast of hot gas and an ear-splitting bang. The monks didn't have much use for this 'black powder' or 'fire medicine', as they called it. But others – who later renamed it gunpowder – sure did!

COOL! WHAT CAN WE BLOW UP NEXT?

THESE MONKS ARE CRAZY!

Trial and error
Some monks reported that as a result of mixing 'fire medicine' their hands and faces were scorched and the houses they were working in burned down. Oops!

trike a light!

ot surprisingly, people at first kept their distance
om the black powder, and it was used mainly for
ending signals. But then some folks began to think
ne explosions were fun. And so fireworks were born.

Bombs away!

More warlike Chinese
realised those bright,
superhot blasts could be
a handy weapon. In the
12th century, military leaders
began making basic rockets,
guns and bombs.

HAVING A BLAST

Experiments proved it was precise
proportions of the ingredients that created
such a powerfully explosive mixture:

75% saltpetre +
15% charcoal +
10% sulphur
= BOOM!

Pulling the trigger

In the 13th century
the Mongols seized
on the new technology and
used it against enemies in West
Asia and Europe. Soon gunpowder
weapons were everywhere. And the
world was never the same again!

In the 10th century
firecrackers were
used to scare away
evil spirits.

LET'S CALL IT...

Chinese names for early weapons were descriptive
and colourful. Link the name to the right definition:

**1. 'Poison-fog magic
smoke eruptor'**

A. A grenade-like bomb
attached to an arrow

**2. 'Flying-sand magic bomb
releasing 10,000 fires'**

B. A cannonball that
released poisonous gas

**3. 'Mysteriously moving,
infantry-breaking fierce-flame
sword-shield'**

C. An explosive pot filled with
sand, sticky resin and liquid
from poisonous plants

**4. 'Fiery pomegranate
shot from a bow'**

D. A huge shield on wheels
through which gunmen could fire

Answers: 1=B; 2=C; 3=D; 4=A.

WANT
MORE?

Early weapons manual ☆ http://history.cultural-china.com/en/37History6314.html

GET LUCKY!

Things not working out the way you hoped? Worried about the future? In China it's thought that there are many ways to boost your fortunes, change things for the better and pave the way to prosperity. It might mean redesigning your house or wearing the right clothes, or simply picking the right numbers – and avoiding the wrong ones!

Dress for success

Forget fashion – choose colours that bring you favour. Red is considered the luckiest colour and is seen everywhere at New Year. Yellow brings good luck too, but white is linked with mourning and therefore misfortune.

LUCKY THERE ARE SIX OF US!

Traditional lucky knot

DO THE NUMBERS

In China, numbers have either good or bad associations, often depending on the words they sound like in Chinese. Link yourself with lucky numbers and steer clear of the dodgy ones.

一 **1** Neutral

二 **2** Usually positive: associated with doubles and pairs

三 **3** Lucky: sounds like the word for 'birth'

四 **4** Oh-oh, the worst number: sounds like 'death'

五 **5** Neither lucky nor unlucky

 6 Lucky: sounds like 'flow'

七 **7** Good for relationships, as it symbolises togetherness

 8 Brings good fortune in business: sounds like 'wealth'

 9 Lucky: linked with emperors and long life

88 CENTS – GEE, THANKS.

ass it on
'ant to pass on your good
ortune? Give a friend some
noney in a lucky red envelope,
hongbao. Make sure the total
um includes an 8 or a 2 – but
ease, no 4s!

Many Chinese buildings
skip floor numbers
containing the number 4.
So there may be no level
4, 14 and so on – or any
at all between 39 and 50!

Put your house in order
For help on the home front,
consult a practitioner of feng shui.
According to this ancient art, the
arrangement of furniture and
doorways is said to affect the flow
of energy and enhance wellbeing.

Stick it up
The Chinese character *fu* means
'luck'. Stick one on your door –
but upside down. That's because
the words for 'upside down' and
'arrives' sound the same in Chinese.
So that way 'luck arrives' – hopefully!

WANT MORE?

The fear of the number 4, which is common in Asia, is called tetraphobia.

INDEX

NOT-FOR-PARENTS
CHINA
EVERYTHING YOU EVER WANTED TO KNOW

1st Edition
Published September 2012

Conceived by Weldon Owen in partnership with Lonely Planet
Produced by Weldon Owen Publishing
Northburgh House, 10 Northburgh Street
London, EC1V 0AT UK

weldonowenpublishing.com

Copyright © 2012 Weldon Owen Publishing

WELDON OWEN LTD

Managing Director Sarah Odedina
Publisher Corinne Roberts
Creative Director Sue Burk
Sales Director Laurence Richard
Sales Manager, North America Ellen Towell
Designer Adam Walker
Design Assistant Haylee Bruce
Index Puddingburn Publishing Services
Production Director Dominic Saraceno
Production Controller Tristan Hanks

Published by
Lonely Planet Publications Pty Ltd ABN 36 005 607 983
90 Maribyrnong St, Footscray, Victoria 3011, Australia

ISBN 978-1-74321-426-8

Printed in China

A WELDON OWEN PRODUCTION

Credits and acknowledgments

Key tl=top left; tcl=top center left; tc=top center; tcr=top center right;
tr=top right; cl=center left; c=center; cr=center right; bl=bottom left;
bcl=bottom center left; bc=bottom center; bcr=bottom center right;
br=bottom right; bg = background.

Photographs

40bl, 41tr, 46tr, 47bl, 50bl, 68bcr, 68-69tc, 72-73tc, 75bc, tl, 79cl, 81tc **Alamy**
19cl, 35tl, 42c, 62b, 69cl, 78tr **Bridgeman Art Library;** 8bc, 9br, 11tr, 12tcr,
14c, 16tr, 17tcr, tr, 18bl, 19bc, 20c, cl, 22bc, 23br, 24bc, 25br, tr, 27c, tr, 28bc
cr, 29br, tc, tl, 30-31c, 32cr, 34br, 35bl, tcr, 36tr, 37cr, 39bc, 44cl, cr, 45br, 48c,
49tl, tr, 50-51tr, 51cr, 52c, tr, 53br, 55tl, 56tcl, 57bcl, bcr, tcr, 58cl, 58-59tc,
59br, 60bcl, br, 61br, 62-63tc, 64-65bl, 65bl, br, tl, 66-67bl, 71br, 74bc, cl,
76cr, tr, 77br, 78bc, br, 80bl, tr, 80-81c, 81br, cr, 82br, 84-85c, 85bc, c, tr, 87bl,
c, tc, tr, 89cr, tr, 92-93c, 93br **Corbis;** 8tr, 9cl, 10br, 14tcr, 20tc, 23tr, 32bl,
36-37c, 38c, 43tcl, 45cr, 46cl, 50tc, 51br, 63tr, 66bl, 70tr, 72bc, cl, 74tr, 76bl,
76-77tr, 78cl, 90cl **Getty Images;** 2br, c, 3tc, 10bcl, tr, 16-17bl, 17bc, c, 21br,
23tcl, 24tc, tr, 25tl, 26bc, tcr, 27bl, br, 28bl, 29bc, tc, tl, tr, 30cl, 31bc, c, tr,
33bl, 34cr, 37tc, 40tr, 41tl, 42-43bc, 43cr, 45tr, 48bc, br, 53c, tc, 55br, 56bcl,
58-59cr, 64tcr, 66tr, 67br, cr, tc, 68br, cl, 69cr, 71c, tc, 72bc, 73br, 77bl, cr,
82bl, 83tr, 84cl, 89bl, 90-91bc, 92bc, br, 94br, tc, 95bcl, bcr, bl, br, tcl, tl
iStockphoto.com; 10tcl, 34cl, 35br, 49bc, 62cr, 71bl **Lonely Planet;** 12bcr,
49br **The Picture Desk;** 2bl, 3bc, bl, br, 4c, 6bc, bl, cr, 6-7bcr, 7bcr, bl, tcr, 9c,
tc, tr, 10c, tcr, 11tl, 12bl, 13tc, 15bc, br, tl, tr, 16cl, 18bcr, cl, tcr, tr, 19tr, 20-21c
21cr, tr, 22tr, 23bl, 27tl, 28tr, 29bc, 30bl, 32c, cl, 33br, 34tr, 36cl, 37bl, tr, 38bc,
tr, 39tc, tl, tr, 41bcr, bl, c, 42bl, tc, 43tcr, tr, 44tr, 44-45c, 53cl, tr, 54tr, 54-55bl,
55cl, tr, 56-57c, 57bc, tc, tl, 58bc, 59bc, cl, tr, 60tcl, 61bc, tc, 62cl, 63bc, br, c,
tl, 64tl, 65tr, 66tr, 67cl, tl, 68c, cr, 69br, tc, 71tl, tr, 73bc, 74bcr, tcr, 76c, 77tr,
81tl, 83cr, tr, 84bl, tc, 85r, 86c, 87br, 88bl, tc, 88-89cl, 89tc, 91c, cl, tc, 92cl,
93bl, t, 94bc, bcr, bl, tcr, tr, 95bc, tc, tc **Shutterstock;** 13bcl, br, tcl, 15bl, cl,
17tl, 20bc, 39c, 46-47bc, 50c, 61bl, 82tr, 83br, 86bl, 86-87tc **Topfoto.**

All repeated frames and image motifs courtesy of **iStockphoto.com**

Illustrations

Cover illustrations by **Chris Corr.**

73tc **Paul Bachem;** 4-5c, 94bcl, 95tr **Chris Corr;** 70bc **Rob Davis/The
Art Agency;** 11bc, 32-33tr, 40c **Geri Ford/The Art Agency;** 72bl, 73tr
Tony Gibbons/Bernard Thornton Artists UK; 47cr **Dave Smith/The
Art Agency**

All illustrations and maps copyright 2012 Weldon Owen Publishing

LONELY PLANET OFFICES

Australia Head Office
Locked Bag 1, Footscray, Victoria 3011
Phone 03 8379 8000 Fax 03 8379 8111

USA
150 Linden St, Oakland, CA 94607
Phone 510 250 6400 Toll free 800 275 8555 Fax 510 893 8572

UK
Media Centre, 201 Wood Lane, London W12 7TQ
Phone 020 8433 1333 Fax 020 8702 0112

lonelyplanet.com/contact